The Ultimate Spelling List (Book 1):

Most Common and Important Spoken and Written Words In English

- Comprehensive Daily Practise Word Lists For Primary School -

Shenouda Makarie

Lifelong Education

1st Edition
2015

Makarie, Shenouda
The Ultimate Spelling List (Book 1): Most Common and Important Spoken and Written Words In English. Comprehensive Daily Practise Word Lists For Primary School

National Library of Australia Cataloguing-in-Publication entry
Creator: Makarie, Shenouda, author.
Title: The ultimate spelling list : most common and important spoken and written words in English : comprehensive daily practise word lists for primary school. Book 1 / Shenouda Makarie.
ISBN: 9780994283641 (paperback)
Target Audience: For primary school age.
Subjects: English language--Orthography and spelling--Problems, exercises, etc.--Juvenile literature. English language--Orthography and spelling--Study and teaching (Primary) Spellers--Juvenile literature.
Dewey Number: 372.632

First Printing: 2015
ISBN 978-0-9942836-4-1

Lifelong Education Series
Other Titles available:
• The Ultimate Spelling List (Book 2): Most Common and Important Spoken and Written Words In English
• Times Tables (Book 1): Comprehensive Memorisation Program with Exercises, Tables 1-6
• Times Tables (Book 2): Comprehensive Memorisation Program with Exercises, Tables 7-12
• Multiplication & Division (Book 1): Comprehensive Mental Exercises, Tables 1-12

Sydney, NSW 2000 – Australia
books@lifelongeducation.com.au
For enquiries or further copies of this book, visit: www.lifelongeducation.com.au

CONTENTS

INTRODUCTION

These days more than ever it is difficult for parents, teachers and tutors to create word lists that are both relevant and important to a child. The spelling words included in this book are **carefully researched and selected from a large worldwide, genre-balanced and up-to-date corpus of contemporary English** – reflecting the **most common and important** spoken and written words in the English language.

This is an incredibly powerful tool! It will enable children to quickly build up a vocabulary that is sound and highly relevant. All in all, these word lists will assist in developing comprehension and communication skills in English.

Beautifully laid out and set out over **2 volumes with 4,800 words**, both books contain comprehensive daily practise **word lists** for primary school children. Children are encouraged to look up the meanings and usage of the words in the dictionary to further enhance their learning.

Daily practise, repetition and structured exposure to new words are critical in helping improve a child's spelling and vocabulary throughout their primary years.

To get the most out of this book, ensure your child completes in order,
at least one set every week, practising daily.

Take charge now, and with the help of these unique comprehensive books, your child will reap the benefits throughout their school years and beyond!

Happy learning,

Sm

Shenouda Makarie

SET 1

Word List

oral	**reply**	**decide**	**tap**	**eye**
sick	**rough**	**town**	**taste**	**cast**
absorb	**while**	**tune**	**smart**	**wire**

INSTRUCTIONS: Review the word list above and then cover. Have someone read out each word while you write them in the spaces below. Review any misspelt words 3 times.

LOOK.   SAY.   COVER.   WRITE.   CHECK.

Practise

Practise 1

Practise 2

Practise 3

TIP Remember, look up each word in your dictionary to learn its meaning!

Need extra practise?
Printable blank practise sheet available from: www.lifelongeducation.com.au/spelling_practise_sheet
(also available on page 167)

SET 2

Date: ....

Word List

tone	apply	often	compel	oven
grip	flood	middle	local	settle
garage	echo	class	sense	broker

INSTRUCTIONS: Review the word list above and then cover. Have someone read out each word while you write them in the spaces below. Review any misspelt words 3 times.

LOOK. SAY. COVER. WRITE. CHECK.

Practise

Practise 1

Practise 2

Practise 3

TIP Remember, look up each word in your dictionary to learn its meaning!

Need extra practise?
Printable blank practise sheet available from: www.lifelongeducation.com.au/spelling_practise_sheet
(also available on page 167)

SET 3

Word List

user	beef	bonus	age	and
August	female	bag	fame	fist
month	split	pack	aid	budget

INSTRUCTIONS: Review the word list above and then cover. Have someone read out each word while you write them in the spaces below. Review any misspelt words 3 times.

LOOK.   SAY.   COVER.   WRITE.   CHECK.

Practise

Practise 1

Practise 2

Practise 3

TIP Remember, look up each word in your dictionary to learn its meaning!

Need extra practise?
Printable blank practise sheet available from: www.lifelongeducation.com.au/spelling_practise_sheet
(also available on page 167)

SET 4

Date: ....

Word List

boss	peer	chaos	rise	surely
fluid	tape	vessel	coal	fully
bread	cook	irony	please	stay

INSTRUCTIONS: Review the word list above and then cover. Have someone read out each word while you write them in the spaces below. Review any misspelt words 3 times.

LOOK.   SAY.   COVER.   WRITE.   CHECK.

Practise

Practise 1

Practise 2

Practise 3

TIP Remember, look up each word in your dictionary to learn its meaning!

Need extra practise?
Printable blank practise sheet available from: www.lifelongeducation.com.au/spelling_practise_sheet
(also available on page 167)

SET 5

Date: ....

Word List

stop	shame	seal	grasp	aware
preach	arrive	county	menu	weaken
wall	need	cope	pair	chain

INSTRUCTIONS: Review the word list above and then cover. Have someone read out each word while you write them in the spaces below. Review any misspelt words 3 times.

LOOK.   SAY.   COVER.   WRITE.   CHECK.

Practise

Practise 1

Practise 2

Practise 3

TIP Remember, look up each word in your dictionary to learn its meaning!

Need extra practise?
Printable blank practise sheet available from: www.lifelongeducation.com.au/spelling_practise_sheet
(also available on page 167)

The Ultimate Spelling List (Book 1): Most Common and Important Spoken and Written Words in English

SET 6

Word List

any	**Friday**	**vacuum**	**bath**	**coast**
unite	**sixth**	**put**	**intact**	**miss**
spring	**wrist**	**ideal**	**silk**	**purple**

INSTRUCTIONS: Review the word list above and then cover. Have someone read out each word while you write them in the spaces below. Review any misspelt words 3 times.

LOOK.   SAY.   COVER.   WRITE.   CHECK.

Practise

Practise 1

Practise 2

Practise 3

TIP Remember, look up each word in your dictionary to learn its meaning!

Need extra practise?
Printable blank practise sheet available from: www.lifelongeducation.com.au/spelling_practise_sheet
(also available on page 167)

SET 7

Word List

singer	**wrong**	**edge**	**health**	**booth**
flight	**sugar**	**oil**	**slow**	**road**
yes	**method**	**weight**	**unfair**	**less**

INSTRUCTIONS: Review the word list above and then cover. Have someone read out each word while you write them in the spaces below. Review any misspelt words 3 times.

LOOK.   SAY.   COVER.   WRITE.   CHECK.

Practise

Practise 1

Practise 2

Practise 3

TIP   Remember, look up each word in your dictionary to learn its meaning!

Need extra practise?
Printable blank practise sheet available from: www.lifelongeducation.com.au/spelling_practise_sheet
(also available on page 167)

SET 8

Date: ....

Word List

mind	spark	tale	tuck	effort
slam	brick	ensure	margin	legal
pat	lower	little	funny	market

INSTRUCTIONS: Review the word list above and then cover. Have someone read out each word while you write them in the spaces below. Review any misspelt words 3 times.

LOOK.   SAY.   COVER.   WRITE.   CHECK.

Practise

Practise 1

Practise 2

Practise 3

TIP Remember, look up each word in your dictionary to learn its meaning!

Need extra practise?
Printable blank practise sheet available from: www.lifelongeducation.com.au/spelling_practise_sheet
(also available on page 167)

Word List

area	paint	sound	marble	eating
orange	flavour	stream	quit	better
listen	kid	throat	forty	melt

INSTRUCTIONS: Review the word list above and then cover. Have someone read out each word while you write them in the spaces below. Review any misspelt words 3 times.

LOOK.   SAY.   COVER.   WRITE.   CHECK.

Practise

Practise 1

Practise 2

Practise 3

TIP Remember, look up each word in your dictionary to learn its meaning!

Need extra practise?
Printable blank practise sheet available from: www.lifelongeducation.com.au/spelling_practise_sheet
(also available on page 167)

SET 10

Date: ....

Word List

come	dawn	curve	closed	ought
father	retail	unlike	shore	sink
growth	trade	island	virtue	likely

INSTRUCTIONS: Review the word list above and then cover. Have someone read out each word while you write them in the spaces below. Review any misspelt words 3 times.

LOOK.   SAY.   COVER.   WRITE.   CHECK.

Practise

Practise 1

Practise 2

Practise 3

TIP: Remember, look up each word in your dictionary to learn its meaning!

Need extra practise?
Printable blank practise sheet available from: www.lifelongeducation.com.au/spelling_practise_sheet
(also available on page 167)

SET 11

Date: ....

Word List

lonely	poll	phrase	bunch	study
value	ankle	rose	garlic	intend
book	buy	fear	left	shine

INSTRUCTIONS: Review the word list above and then cover. Have someone read out each word while you write them in the spaces below. Review any misspelt words 3 times.

LOOK.   SAY.   COVER.   WRITE.   CHECK.

Practise

Practise 1

Practise 2

Practise 3

TIP Remember, look up each word in your dictionary to learn its meaning!

Need extra practise?
Printable blank practise sheet available from: www.lifelongeducation.com.au/spelling_practise_sheet
(also available on page 167)

The Ultimate Spelling List (Book 1): Most Common and Important Spoken and Written Words in English

SET 12

Date: ....

Word List

sand	wet	snap	neck	ask
shall	boost	title	humor	such
squad	straw	tough	cash	eleven

INSTRUCTIONS: Review the word list above and then cover. Have someone read out each word while you write them in the spaces below. Review any misspelt words 3 times.

LOOK.   SAY.   COVER.   WRITE.   CHECK.

Practise

Practise 1

Practise 2

Practise 3

TIP Remember, look up each word in your dictionary to learn its meaning!

Need extra practise?
Printable blank practise sheet available from: www.lifelongeducation.com.au/spelling_practise_sheet
(also available on page 167)

The Ultimate Spelling List (Book 1): Most Common and Important Spoken and Written Words in English   **17**

SET 13

Word List

major	trust	empire	tissue	glance
accept	cat	limb	hang	coach
kill	easily	pass	silver	garden

INSTRUCTIONS: Review the word list above and then cover. Have someone read out each word while you write them in the spaces below. Review any misspelt words 3 times.

LOOK.   SAY.   COVER.   WRITE.   CHECK.

Practise

Practise 1

Practise 2

Practise 3

TIP Remember, look up each word in your dictionary to learn its meaning!

Need extra practise?
Printable blank practise sheet available from: www.lifelongeducation.com.au/spelling_practise_sheet
(also available on page 167)

SET 14

Word List

secure	engage	fourth	state	proud
pizza	luck	rating	maker	odds
beside	fat	blast	rubber	phone

INSTRUCTIONS: Review the word list above and then cover. Have someone read out each word while you write them in the spaces below. Review any misspelt words 3 times.

LOOK.   SAY.   COVER.   WRITE.   CHECK.

Practise

Practise 1

Practise 2

Practise 3

TIP Remember, look up each word in your dictionary to learn its meaning!

Need extra practise?
Printable blank practise sheet available from: www.lifelongeducation.com.au/spelling_practise_sheet
(also available on page 167)

Date: ....

Word List

solve	dock	plunge	afford	glove
check	admit	worker	east	mall
craft	alley	organ	client	ash

INSTRUCTIONS: Review the word list above and then cover. Have someone read out each word while you write them in the spaces below. Review any misspelt words 3 times.

LOOK.   SAY.   COVER.   WRITE.   CHECK.

Practise

Practise 1

Practise 2

Practise 3

TIP Remember, look up each word in your dictionary to learn its meaning!

Need extra practise?
Printable blank practise sheet available from: www.lifelongeducation.com.au/spelling_practise_sheet
(also available on page 167)

Date: ....

Word List

mine	around	spirit	cure	drunk
pine	can	slowly	denial	than
horror	whip	gate	grand	must

INSTRUCTIONS: Review the word list above and then cover. Have someone read out each word while you write them in the spaces below. Review any misspelt words 3 times.

LOOK.   SAY.   COVER.   WRITE.   CHECK.

Practise

Practise 1

Practise 2

Practise 3

TIP Remember, look up each word in your dictionary to learn its meaning!

Need extra practise?
Printable blank practise sheet available from: www.lifelongeducation.com.au/spelling_practise_sheet
(also available on page 167)

SET 17

Date: ....

Word List

lab	armed	post	coin	quick
pocket	want	awake	album	rush
accuse	beyond	window	return	domain

INSTRUCTIONS: Review the word list above and then cover. Have someone read out each word while you write them in the spaces below. Review any misspelt words 3 times.

LOOK. SAY. COVER. WRITE. CHECK.

Practise

Practise 1

Practise 2

Practise 3

⬡ TIP Remember, look up each word in your dictionary to learn its meaning!

Need extra practise?
Printable blank practise sheet available from: www.lifelongeducation.com.au/spelling_practise_sheet
(also available on page 167)

SET 18

Word List

moral	launch	say	dirt	crisis
target	cost	unable	fold	letter
reveal	scheme	part	twice	woman

INSTRUCTIONS: Review the word list above and then cover. Have someone read out each word while you write them in the spaces below. Review any misspelt words 3 times.

LOOK. SAY. COVER. WRITE. CHECK.

Practise

Practise 1

Practise 2

Practise 3

TIP Remember, look up each word in your dictionary to learn its meaning!

Need extra practise?
Printable blank practise sheet available from: www.lifelongeducation.com.au/spelling_practise_sheet
(also available on page 167)

SET 19

Word List

uncle	break	single	arrow	seek
cut	nest	scan	inmate	they
aisle	chief	gather	bishop	ease

INSTRUCTIONS: Review the word list above and then cover. Have someone read out each word while you write them in the spaces below. Review any misspelt words 3 times.

LOOK.   SAY.   COVER.   WRITE.   CHECK.

Practise

Practise 1

Practise 2

Practise 3

TIP Remember, look up each word in your dictionary to learn its meaning!

Need extra practise?
Printable blank practise sheet available from: www.lifelongeducation.com.au/spelling_practise_sheet
(also available on page 167)

SET 20

Date: ....

Word List

outer	peanut	prison	trail	cancer
square	raise	refuge	elect	wisdom
fellow	wish	public	bullet	dear

INSTRUCTIONS: Review the word list above and then cover. Have someone read out each word while you write them in the spaces below. Review any misspelt words 3 times.

LOOK.   SAY.   COVER.   WRITE.   CHECK.

Practise

Practise 1

Practise 2

Practise 3

TIP Remember, look up each word in your dictionary to learn its meaning!

Need extra practise?
Printable blank practise sheet available from: www.lifelongeducation.com.au/spelling_practise_sheet
(also available on page 167)

SET 21

Date: ....

Word List

lead	begin	Sunday	habit	drain
dam	sleeve	touch	enemy	reach
entire	exotic	swell	equip	metre

INSTRUCTIONS: Review the word list above and then cover. Have someone read out each word while you write them in the spaces below. Review any misspelt words 3 times.

LOOK.   SAY.   COVER.   WRITE.   CHECK.

Practise

Practise 1

Practise 2

Practise 3

TIP Remember, look up each word in your dictionary to learn its meaning!

Need extra practise?
Printable blank practise sheet available from: www.lifelongeducation.com.au/spelling_practise_sheet
(also available on page 167)

The Ultimate Spelling List (Book 1): Most Common and Important Spoken and Written Words in English

SET 22

Word List

derive	priest	punish	shock	stance
widow	faster	dish	update	tree
powder	theme	comedy	rocket	yield

INSTRUCTIONS: Review the word list above and then cover. Have someone read out each word while you write them in the spaces below. Review any misspelt words 3 times.

LOOK.   SAY.   COVER.   WRITE.   CHECK.

Practise

Practise 1

Practise 2

Practise 3

TIP Remember, look up each word in your dictionary to learn its meaning!

Need extra practise?
Printable blank practise sheet available from: www.lifelongeducation.com.au/spelling_practise_sheet
(also available on page 167)

SET 23

Date: ....

Word List

what	remain	shove	ear	table
labour	steel	extend	lean	world
kit	lion	pulse	bubble	like

INSTRUCTIONS: Review the word list above and then cover. Have someone read out each word while you write them in the spaces below. Review any misspelt words 3 times.

LOOK.   SAY.   COVER.   WRITE.   CHECK.

Practise

Practise 1

Practise 2

Practise 3

TIP Remember, look up each word in your dictionary to learn its meaning!

Need extra practise?
Printable blank practise sheet available from: www.lifelongeducation.com.au/spelling_practise_sheet
(also available on page 167)

SET 24

Word List

agency	subtle	intent	sack	tire
heavy	fifth	crop	salmon	source
float	crowd	boom	way	seed

INSTRUCTIONS: Review the word list above and then cover. Have someone read out each word while you write them in the spaces below. Review any misspelt words 3 times.

LOOK.   SAY.   COVER.   WRITE.   CHECK.

Practise

Practise 1

Practise 2

Practise 3

TIP Remember, look up each word in your dictionary to learn its meaning!

Need extra practise?
Printable blank practise sheet available from: www.lifelongeducation.com.au/spelling_practise_sheet
(also available on page 167)

SET 25

Word List

case	mild	her	action	hope
one	device	near	angel	heel
belt	those	dust	key	spite

INSTRUCTIONS: Review the word list above and then cover. Have someone read out each word while you write them in the spaces below. Review any misspelt words 3 times.

LOOK. SAY. COVER. WRITE. CHECK.

Practise

Practise 1

Practise 2

Practise 3

TIP Remember, look up each word in your dictionary to learn its meaning!

Need extra practise?
Printable blank practise sheet available from: www.lifelongeducation.com.au/spelling_practise_sheet
(also available on page 167)

SET 26

Word List

lip	jury	gut	random	scope
fine	dark	survey	not	their
wolf	rod	regain	hit	year

INSTRUCTIONS: Review the word list above and then cover. Have someone read out each word while you write them in the spaces below. Review any misspelt words 3 times.

LOOK.   SAY.   COVER.   WRITE.   CHECK.

Practise

Practise 1

Practise 2

Practise 3

TIP Remember, look up each word in your dictionary to learn its meaning!

Need extra practise?
Printable blank practise sheet available from: www.lifelongeducation.com.au/spelling_practise_sheet
(also available on page 167)

SET 27

Word List

buddy	donor	crack	boy	resort
blue	beast	debt	latter	crush
bill	within	sale	lovely	hip

INSTRUCTIONS: Review the word list above and then cover. Have someone read out each word while you write them in the spaces below. Review any misspelt words 3 times.

LOOK.   SAY.   COVER.   WRITE.   CHECK.

Practise

Practise 1

Practise 2

Practise 3

TIP Remember, look up each word in your dictionary to learn its meaning!

Need extra practise?
Printable blank practise sheet available from: www.lifelongeducation.com.au/spelling_practise_sheet
(also available on page 167)

SET 28

Date: ....

Word List

catch	potato	power	parade	belly
collar	prime	boil	group	duck
beat	enable	blow	doctor	dose

INSTRUCTIONS: Review the word list above and then cover. Have someone read out each word while you write them in the spaces below. Review any misspelt words 3 times.

LOOK.   SAY.   COVER.   WRITE.   CHECK.

Practise

Practise 1

Practise 2

Practise 3

(TIP) Remember, look up each word in your dictionary to learn its meaning!

Need extra practise?
Printable blank practise sheet available from: www.lifelongeducation.com.au/spelling_practise_sheet
(also available on page 167)

SET 29

Word List

bull	summer	pool	weigh	troop
cute	dare	heat	seven	gold
invent	advise	hard	mask	drawer

INSTRUCTIONS: Review the word list above and then cover. Have someone read out each word while you write them in the spaces below. Review any misspelt words 3 times.

LOOK.   SAY.   COVER.   WRITE.   CHECK.

Practise

Practise 1

Practise 2

Practise 3

TIP Remember, look up each word in your dictionary to learn its meaning!

Need extra practise?
Printable blank practise sheet available from: www.lifelongeducation.com.au/spelling_practise_sheet
(also available on page 167)

SET 30

Word List

foot	**roll**	**drove**	**home**	**join**
speech	**person**	**dress**	**saving**	**yell**
medium	**suburb**	**lung**	**stiff**	**enact**

INSTRUCTIONS: Review the word list above and then cover. Have someone read out each word while you write them in the spaces below. Review any misspelt words 3 times.

LOOK.   SAY.   COVER.   WRITE.   CHECK.

Practise

Practise 1

Practise 2

Practise 3

TIP Remember, look up each word in your dictionary to learn its meaning!

Need extra practise?
Printable blank practise sheet available from: www.lifelongeducation.com.au/spelling_practise_sheet
(also available on page 167)

SET 31

Word List

loose	battle	rid	truth	draft
leg	juice	fence	crew	lake
period	test	hot	play	anyway

INSTRUCTIONS: Review the word list above and then cover. Have someone read out each word while you write them in the spaces below. Review any misspelt words 3 times.

LOOK.   SAY.   COVER.   WRITE.   CHECK.

Practise

Practise 1

Practise 2

Practise 3

TIP Remember, look up each word in your dictionary to learn its meaning!

Need extra practise?
Printable blank practise sheet available from: www.lifelongeducation.com.au/spelling_practise_sheet
(also available on page 167)

SET 32

Word List

loyal	beard	parent	away	pit
border	snack	forget	clinic	rabbit
wear	shrimp	pad	gray	legacy

INSTRUCTIONS: Review the word list above and then cover. Have someone read out each word while you write them in the spaces below. Review any misspelt words 3 times.

LOOK.   SAY.   COVER.   WRITE.   CHECK.

Practise

Practise 1

Practise 2

Practise 3

TIP Remember, look up each word in your dictionary to learn its meaning!

Need extra practise?
Printable blank practise sheet available from: www.lifelongeducation.com.au/spelling_practise_sheet
(also available on page 167)

SET 33

Date: ....

Word List

patrol	double	later	myth	tail
sail	disc	insert	sign	rich
sad	decade	auto	jeans	gain

INSTRUCTIONS: Review the word list above and then cover. Have someone read out each word while you write them in the spaces below. Review any misspelt words 3 times.

LOOK.   SAY.   COVER.   WRITE.   CHECK.

Practise

Practise 1

Practise 2

Practise 3

TIP Remember, look up each word in your dictionary to learn its meaning!

Need extra practise?
Printable blank practise sheet available from: www.lifelongeducation.com.au/spelling_practise_sheet
(also available on page 167)

SET 34

Word List

sudden	huge	adjust	topic	camera
grave	rain	bug	sport	beach
racism	build	past	famous	argue

INSTRUCTIONS: Review the word list above and then cover. Have someone read out each word while you write them in the spaces below. Review any misspelt words 3 times.

LOOK.   SAY.   COVER.   WRITE.   CHECK.

Practise

Practise 1

Practise 2

Practise 3

TIP Remember, look up each word in your dictionary to learn its meaning!

Need extra practise?
Printable blank practise sheet available from: www.lifelongeducation.com.au/spelling_practise_sheet
(also available on page 167)

SET 35

Date: ....

Word List

era	strong	select	hardly	teen
repair	walk	alone	porch	react
death	bitter	visit	salary	whale

INSTRUCTIONS: Review the word list above and then cover. Have someone read out each word while you write them in the spaces below. Review any misspelt words 3 times.

LOOK.   SAY.   COVER.   WRITE.   CHECK.

Practise

Practise 1

Practise 2

Practise 3

TIP Remember, look up each word in your dictionary to learn its meaning!

Need extra practise?
Printable blank practise sheet available from: www.lifelongeducation.com.au/spelling_practise_sheet
(also available on page 167)

The Ultimate Spelling List (Book 1): Most Common and Important Spoken and Written Words in English

SET 36

Date: ....

Word List

clean	tiger	drill	talk	adapt
brand	friend	six	line	brain
winter	pale	lift	inform	pen

INSTRUCTIONS: Review the word list above and then cover. Have someone read out each word while you write them in the spaces below. Review any misspelt words 3 times.

LOOK.   SAY.   COVER.   WRITE.   CHECK.

Practise

Practise 1

Practise 2

Practise 3

TIP Remember, look up each word in your dictionary to learn its meaning!

Need extra practise?
Printable blank practise sheet available from: www.lifelongeducation.com.au/spelling_practise_sheet
(also available on page 167)

Date: ....

Word List

cycle	thus	rental	honey	care
tragic	radar	poster	mutual	except
front	fibre	whom	eat	once

INSTRUCTIONS: Review the word list above and then cover. Have someone read out each word while you write them in the spaces below. Review any misspelt words 3 times.

LOOK.   SAY.   COVER.   WRITE.   CHECK.

Practise

Practise 1

Practise 2

Practise 3

TIP Remember, look up each word in your dictionary to learn its meaning!

Need extra practise?
Printable blank practise sheet available from: www.lifelongeducation.com.au/spelling_practise_sheet
(also available on page 167)

SET 38

Word List

storm	born	ruling	alien	appear
king	ready	sock	least	misery
far	wipe	life	from	closet

INSTRUCTIONS: Review the word list above and then cover. Have someone read out each word while you write them in the spaces below. Review any misspelt words 3 times.

LOOK.   SAY.   COVER.   WRITE.   CHECK.

Practise

Practise 1

Practise 2

Practise 3

TIP Remember, look up each word in your dictionary to learn its meaning!

Need extra practise?
Printable blank practise sheet available from: www.lifelongeducation.com.au/spelling_practise_sheet
(also available on page 167)

SET 39

Word List

holy	excuse	alarm	code	force
regret	bush	tumour	fatal	knife
lesson	kind	relief	guide	toxic

INSTRUCTIONS: Review the word list above and then cover. Have someone read out each word while you write them in the spaces below. Review any misspelt words 3 times.

LOOK.   SAY.   COVER.   WRITE.   CHECK.

Practise

Practise 1

Practise 2

Practise 3

TIP Remember, look up each word in your dictionary to learn its meaning!

Need extra practise?
Printable blank practise sheet available from: www.lifelongeducation.com.au/spelling_practise_sheet
(also available on page 167)

SET 40

Word List

soul	deep	pursue	mix	die
former	accent	opera	view	make
result	endure	rare	car	piano

INSTRUCTIONS: Review the word list above and then cover. Have someone read out each word while you write them in the spaces below. Review any misspelt words 3 times.

LOOK.   SAY.   COVER.   WRITE.   CHECK.

Practise

Practise 1

Practise 2

Practise 3

TIP Remember, look up each word in your dictionary to learn its meaning!

Need extra practise?
Printable blank practise sheet available from: www.lifelongeducation.com.au/spelling_practise_sheet
(also available on page 167)

SET 41

Word List

panel	cloud	piece	still	issue
burden	casino	afraid	gender	trunk
ladder	senior	affect	day	voice

INSTRUCTIONS: Review the word list above and then cover. Have someone read out each word while you write them in the spaces below. Review any misspelt words 3 times.

LOOK.   SAY.   COVER.   WRITE.   CHECK.

Practise

Practise 1

Practise 2

Practise 3

TIP Remember, look up each word in your dictionary to learn its meaning!

Need extra practise?
Printable blank practise sheet available from: www.lifelongeducation.com.au/spelling_practise_sheet
(also available on page 167)

SET 42

Word List

gross	ratio	deny	army	sweep
apart	fate	heal	simple	centre
voter	white	never	rat	moment

INSTRUCTIONS: Review the word list above and then cover. Have someone read out each word while you write them in the spaces below. Review any misspelt words 3 times.

LOOK.   SAY.   COVER.   WRITE.   CHECK.

Practise

Practise 1

Practise 2

Practise 3

⬡ TIP Remember, look up each word in your dictionary to learn its meaning!

Need extra practise?
Printable blank practise sheet available from: www.lifelongeducation.com.au/spelling_practise_sheet
(also available on page 167)

SET 43

Word List

lane	heaven	bounce	smooth	profit
dip	match	switch	tackle	spend
basis	foster	rate	July	mud

INSTRUCTIONS: Review the word list above and then cover. Have someone read out each word while you write them in the spaces below. Review any misspelt words 3 times.

LOOK.   SAY.   COVER.   WRITE.   CHECK.

Practise

Practise 1

Practise 2

Practise 3

(TIP) Remember, look up each word in your dictionary to learn its meaning!

Need extra practise?
Printable blank practise sheet available from: www.lifelongeducation.com.au/spelling_practise_sheet
(also available on page 167)

SET 44

Word List

sword	trick	dirty	wound	hand
police	money	tag	that	excel
system	loud	known	you	remark

INSTRUCTIONS: Review the word list above and then cover. Have someone read out each word while you write them in the spaces below. Review any misspelt words 3 times.

LOOK.   SAY.   COVER.   WRITE.   CHECK.

Practise

Practise 1

Practise 2

Practise 3

TIP Remember, look up each word in your dictionary to learn its meaning!

Need extra practise?
Printable blank practise sheet available from: www.lifelongeducation.com.au/spelling_practise_sheet
(also available on page 167)

Date: ....

Word List

prior	recall	agent	brake	space
jacket	weak	ugly	over	design
tender	war	driver	tongue	rest

INSTRUCTIONS: Review the word list above and then cover. Have someone read out each word while you write them in the spaces below. Review any misspelt words 3 times.

LOOK.   SAY.   COVER.   WRITE.   CHECK.

Practise

Practise 1

Practise 2

Practise 3

TIP Remember, look up each word in your dictionary to learn its meaning!

Need extra practise?
Printable blank practise sheet available from: www.lifelongeducation.com.au/spelling_practise_sheet
(also available on page 167)

SET 46

Date: ....

Word List

spare	critic	glass	vital	twist
medal	also	haul	price	till
amount	chip	might	cell	scent

INSTRUCTIONS: Review the word list above and then cover. Have someone read out each word while you write them in the spaces below. Review any misspelt words 3 times.

LOOK.   SAY.   COVER.   WRITE.   CHECK.

Practise

Practise 1

Practise 2

Practise 3

TIP Remember, look up each word in your dictionary to learn its meaning!

Need extra practise?
Printable blank practise sheet available from: www.lifelongeducation.com.au/spelling_practise_sheet
(also available on page 167)

The Ultimate Spelling List (Book 1): Most Common and Important Spoken and Written Words in English   **51**

SET 47

Date: ....

Word List

thanks	whole	swift	fork	genius
card	ball	deal	flour	warm
icon	alter	thirty	keep	govern

INSTRUCTIONS: Review the word list above and then cover. Have someone read out each word while you write them in the spaces below. Review any misspelt words 3 times.

LOOK. SAY. COVER. WRITE. CHECK.

Practise

Practise 1

Practise 2

Practise 3

TIP Remember, look up each word in your dictionary to learn its meaning!

Need extra practise?
Printable blank practise sheet available from: www.lifelongeducation.com.au/spelling_practise_sheet
(also available on page 167)

SET 48

Word List

sorry	sum	before	stable	ever
sigh	your	stare	bottle	vision
fault	aussie	depict	drink	toilet

INSTRUCTIONS: Review the word list above and then cover. Have someone read out each word while you write them in the spaces below. Review any misspelt words 3 times.

LOOK.   SAY.   COVER.   WRITE.   CHECK.

Practise

Practise 1

Practise 2

Practise 3

TIP Remember, look up each word in your dictionary to learn its meaning!

Need extra practise?
Printable blank practise sheet available from: www.lifelongeducation.com.au/spelling_practise_sheet
(also available on page 167)

SET 49

Word List

seize	jail	charm	mark	lamp
impact	patent	legend	suck	shrink
openly	grow	grin	fee	soap

INSTRUCTIONS: Review the word list above and then cover. Have someone read out each word while you write them in the spaces below. Review any misspelt words 3 times.

LOOK.   SAY.   COVER.   WRITE.   CHECK.

Practise

Practise 1

Practise 2

Practise 3

TIP Remember, look up each word in your dictionary to learn its meaning!

Need extra practise?
Printable blank practise sheet available from: www.lifelongeducation.com.au/spelling_practise_sheet
(also available on page 167)

SET 50

Word List

income	**danger**	**temple**	**usual**	**great**
egg	**work**	**editor**	**real**	**depart**
tide	**fall**	**shop**	**farm**	**hat**

INSTRUCTIONS: Review the word list above and then cover. Have someone read out each word while you write them in the spaces below. Review any misspelt words 3 times.

LOOK.   SAY.   COVER.   WRITE.   CHECK.

Practise

Practise 1

Practise 2

Practise 3

TIP Remember, look up each word in your dictionary to learn its meaning!

Need extra practise?
Printable blank practise sheet available from: www.lifelongeducation.com.au/spelling_practise_sheet
(also available on page 167)

SET 51

Date: ....

Word List

senate	dot	attire	resist	pain
sky	patch	factor	custom	actual
bulb	expose	pet	hidden	pick

INSTRUCTIONS: Review the word list above and then cover. Have someone read out each word while you write them in the spaces below. Review any misspelt words 3 times.

LOOK.   SAY.   COVER.   WRITE.   CHECK.

Practise

Practise 1

Practise 2

Practise 3

TIP Remember, look up each word in your dictionary to learn its meaning!

Need extra practise?
Printable blank practise sheet available from: www.lifelongeducation.com.au/spelling_practise_sheet
(also available on page 167)

SET 52

Date: ....

Word List

gift	man	detect	lover	golden
sheet	shark	annoy	sample	moon
vendor	forbid	exact	Bible	team

INSTRUCTIONS: Review the word list above and then cover. Have someone read out each word while you write them in the spaces below. Review any misspelt words 3 times.

LOOK.   SAY.   COVER.   WRITE.   CHECK.

Practise

Practise 1

Practise 2

Practise 3

TIP Remember, look up each word in your dictionary to learn its meaning!

Need extra practise?
Printable blank practise sheet available from: www.lifelongeducation.com.au/spelling_practise_sheet
(also available on page 167)

SET 53

Word List

devote	page	behave	most	locate
stir	drug	same	giant	dog
shelf	him	inside	Sydney	pond

INSTRUCTIONS: Review the word list above and then cover. Have someone read out each word while you write them in the spaces below. Review any misspelt words 3 times.

LOOK.   SAY.   COVER.   WRITE.   CHECK.

Practise

Practise 1

Practise 2

Practise 3

(TIP) Remember, look up each word in your dictionary to learn its meaning!

Need extra practise?
Printable blank practise sheet available from: www.lifelongeducation.com.au/spelling_practise_sheet
(also available on page 167)

SET 54

Word List

shy	jet	input	ride	wagon
await	fade	ego	fund	type
whose	mouth	rally	costly	mammal

INSTRUCTIONS: Review the word list above and then cover. Have someone read out each word while you write them in the spaces below. Review any misspelt words 3 times.

LOOK.   SAY.   COVER.   WRITE.   CHECK.

Practise

Practise 1

Practise 2

Practise 3

TIP Remember, look up each word in your dictionary to learn its meaning!

Need extra practise?
Printable blank practise sheet available from: www.lifelongeducation.com.au/spelling_practise_sheet
(also available on page 167)

SET 55

Word List

dry	evolve	cap	colony	them
until	corner	scale	online	spine
drum	just	talent	wheel	rhythm

INSTRUCTIONS: Review the word list above and then cover. Have someone read out each word while you write them in the spaces below. Review any misspelt words 3 times.

LOOK.   SAY.   COVER.   WRITE.   CHECK.

Practise

Practise 1

Practise 2

Practise 3

TIP Remember, look up each word in your dictionary to learn its meaning!

Need extra practise?
Printable blank practise sheet available from: www.lifelongeducation.com.au/spelling_practise_sheet
(also available on page 167)

SET 56

Word List

horn	soil	shirt	bell	floor
pan	freeze	even	guitar	beer
shared	pink	date	dining	racial

INSTRUCTIONS: Review the word list above and then cover. Have someone read out each word while you write them in the spaces below. Review any misspelt words 3 times.

LOOK.   SAY.   COVER.   WRITE.   CHECK.

Practise

Practise 1

Practise 2

Practise 3

TIP Remember, look up each word in your dictionary to learn its meaning!

Need extra practise?
Printable blank practise sheet available from: www.lifelongeducation.com.au/spelling_practise_sheet
(also available on page 167)

SET 57

Word List

relax	apple	joint	belief	circle
down	steady	others	steep	pot
baby	place	notice	amid	monkey

INSTRUCTIONS: Review the word list above and then cover. Have someone read out each word while you write them in the spaces below. Review any misspelt words 3 times.

LOOK.   SAY.   COVER.   WRITE.   CHECK.

Practise

Practise 1

Practise 2

Practise 3

TIP Remember, look up each word in your dictionary to learn its meaning!

Need extra practise?
Printable blank practise sheet available from: www.lifelongeducation.com.au/spelling_practise_sheet
(also available on page 167)

SET 58

Date: ....

Word List

tour	let	round	tax	always
take	about	queen	cite	cliff
arena	error	reject	matter	fifty

INSTRUCTIONS: Review the word list above and then cover. Have someone read out each word while you write them in the spaces below. Review any misspelt words 3 times.

LOOK.   SAY.   COVER.   WRITE.   CHECK.

Practise

Practise 1

Practise 2

Practise 3

TIP Remember, look up each word in your dictionary to learn its meaning!

Need extra practise?
Printable blank practise sheet available from: www.lifelongeducation.com.au/spelling_practise_sheet
(also available on page 167)

SET 59

Word List

else	hint	royal	north	mill
net	with	role	favour	level
seat	guest	tray	side	loan

INSTRUCTIONS: Review the word list above and then cover. Have someone read out each word while you write them in the spaces below. Review any misspelt words 3 times.

LOOK.   SAY.   COVER.   WRITE.   CHECK.

Practise

Practise 1

Practise 2

Practise 3

TIP Remember, look up each word in your dictionary to learn its meaning!

Need extra practise?
Printable blank practise sheet available from: www.lifelongeducation.com.au/spelling_practise_sheet
(also available on page 167)

SET 60

Word List

band	rapid	guard	basket	weed
every	right	carry	plan	dying
city	tear	quest	meal	beauty

INSTRUCTIONS: Review the word list above and then cover. Have someone read out each word while you write them in the spaces below. Review any misspelt words 3 times.

LOOK.   SAY.   COVER.   WRITE.   CHECK.

Practise

Practise 1

Practise 2

Practise 3

TIP Remember, look up each word in your dictionary to learn its meaning!

Need extra practise?
Printable blank practise sheet available from: www.lifelongeducation.com.au/spelling_practise_sheet
(also available on page 167)

SET 61

Word List

forest	move	tomato	art	blonde
cheap	asset	rural	set	bowl
ten	lady	submit	gang	sneak

INSTRUCTIONS: Review the word list above and then cover. Have someone read out each word while you write them in the spaces below. Review any misspelt words 3 times.

LOOK. SAY. COVER. WRITE. CHECK.

Practise

Practise 1

Practise 2

Practise 3

TIP Remember, look up each word in your dictionary to learn its meaning!

Need extra practise?
Printable blank practise sheet available from: www.lifelongeducation.com.au/spelling_practise_sheet
(also available on page 167)

SET 62

Word List

anyone	rage	junior	outlet	flower
family	poke	ocean	wild	beg
forth	season	house	sunny	palm

INSTRUCTIONS: Review the word list above and then cover. Have someone read out each word while you write them in the spaces below. Review any misspelt words 3 times.

LOOK.   SAY.   COVER.   WRITE.   CHECK.

Practise

Practise 1

Practise 2

Practise 3

TIP Remember, look up each word in your dictionary to learn its meaning!

Need extra practise?
Printable blank practise sheet available from: www.lifelongeducation.com.au/spelling_practise_sheet
(also available on page 167)

Date: ....

Word List

suite	occupy	joy	prompt	model
prize	print	devour	below	create
honest	soup	film	breeze	attack

INSTRUCTIONS: Review the word list above and then cover. Have someone read out each word while you write them in the spaces below. Review any misspelt words 3 times.

LOOK.   SAY.   COVER.   WRITE.   CHECK.

Practise

Practise 1

Practise 2

Practise 3

TIP Remember, look up each word in your dictionary to learn its meaning!

Need extra practise?
Printable blank practise sheet available from: www.lifelongeducation.com.au/spelling_practise_sheet
(also available on page 167)

Word List

greet	bank	firmly	radio	today
worth	heart	kiss	paper	avoid
fish	tool	insist	estate	stand

INSTRUCTIONS: Review the word list above and then cover. Have someone read out each word while you write them in the spaces below. Review any misspelt words 3 times.

LOOK.   SAY.   COVER.   WRITE.   CHECK.

Practise

Practise 1

Practise 2

Practise 3

TIP Remember, look up each word in your dictionary to learn its meaning!

Need extra practise?
Printable blank practise sheet available from: www.lifelongeducation.com.au/spelling_practise_sheet
(also available on page 167)

Date: ....

Word List

memory	pop	status	screw	guilty
rice	bomb	short	dance	June
blank	feel	planet	panic	refuse

INSTRUCTIONS: Review the word list above and then cover. Have someone read out each word while you write them in the spaces below. Review any misspelt words 3 times.

LOOK.   SAY.   COVER.   WRITE.   CHECK.

Practise

Practise 1

Practise 2

Practise 3

TIP Remember, look up each word in your dictionary to learn its meaning!

Need extra practise?
Printable blank practise sheet available from: www.lifelongeducation.com.au/spelling_practise_sheet
(also available on page 167)

SET 66

Word List

import	tribe	dealer	cheer	impose
anger	breath	arrest	cross	charge
nor	four	write	climb	bureau

INSTRUCTIONS: Review the word list above and then cover. Have someone read out each word while you write them in the spaces below. Review any misspelt words 3 times.

LOOK.   SAY.   COVER.   WRITE.   CHECK.

Practise

Practise 1

Practise 2

Practise 3

TIP Remember, look up each word in your dictionary to learn its meaning!

Need extra practise?
Printable blank practise sheet available from: www.lifelongeducation.com.au/spelling_practise_sheet
(also available on page 167)

SET 67

Word List

self	**lots**	**render**	**weapon**	**boot**
coming	**treaty**	**tribal**	**wife**	**map**
actor	**output**	**civic**	**annual**	**extra**

INSTRUCTIONS: Review the word list above and then cover. Have someone read out each word while you write them in the spaces below. Review any misspelt words 3 times.

LOOK. SAY. COVER. WRITE. CHECK.

Practise

Practise 1

Practise 2

Practise 3

TIP Remember, look up each word in your dictionary to learn its meaning!

Need extra practise?
Printable blank practise sheet available from: www.lifelongeducation.com.au/spelling_practise_sheet
(also available on page 167)

SET 68

Word List

know	**jazz**	**pay**	**volume**	**final**
lately	**mess**	**pace**	**alike**	**slot**
sea	**chef**	**debris**	**carve**	**metal**

INSTRUCTIONS: Review the word list above and then cover. Have someone read out each word while you write them in the spaces below. Review any misspelt words 3 times.

LOOK.   SAY.   COVER.   WRITE.   CHECK.

Practise

Practise 1

Practise 2

Practise 3

TIP Remember, look up each word in your dictionary to learn its meaning!

Need extra practise?
Printable blank practise sheet available from: www.lifelongeducation.com.au/spelling_practise_sheet
(also available on page 167)

SET 69

Word List

hurt	pepper	sharp	cop	lucky
false	marine	summit	travel	grain
lock	carpet	flesh	exist	assume

INSTRUCTIONS: Review the word list above and then cover. Have someone read out each word while you write them in the spaces below. Review any misspelt words 3 times.

LOOK.   SAY.   COVER.   WRITE.   CHECK.

Practise

Practise 1

Practise 2

Practise 3

TIP Remember, look up each word in your dictionary to learn its meaning!

Need extra practise?
Printable blank practise sheet available from: www.lifelongeducation.com.au/spelling_practise_sheet
(also available on page 167)

SET 70

Date: ....

Word List

ethnic	**assure**	**wood**	**wing**	**gently**
wide	**hike**	**tell**	**casual**	**object**
mount	**remote**	**live**	**girl**	**chop**

INSTRUCTIONS: Review the word list above and then cover. Have someone read out each word while you write them in the spaces below. Review any misspelt words 3 times.

LOOK.   SAY.   COVER.   WRITE.   CHECK.

Practise

Practise 1

Practise 2

Practise 3

TIP Remember, look up each word in your dictionary to learn its meaning!

Need extra practise?
Printable blank practise sheet available from: www.lifelongeducation.com.au/spelling_practise_sheet
(also available on page 167)

SET 71

Date: ....

Word List

orbit	repeat	blood	length	food
couch	lose	scream	dinner	ground
meet	signal	loss	upon	theory

INSTRUCTIONS: Review the word list above and then cover. Have someone read out each word while you write them in the spaces below. Review any misspelt words 3 times.

LOOK. SAY. COVER. WRITE. CHECK.

Practise

Practise 1

Practise 2

Practise 3

TIP> Remember, look up each word in your dictionary to learn its meaning!

Need extra practise?
Printable blank practise sheet available from: www.lifelongeducation.com.au/spelling_practise_sheet
(also available on page 167)

The Ultimate Spelling List (Book 1): Most Common and Important Spoken and Written Words in English

SET 72

Word List

number	hero	flat	rule	adopt
pour	rule	fued	pour	buyer
delay	out	ribbon	used	seller

INSTRUCTIONS: Review the word list above and then cover. Have someone read out each word while you write them in the spaces below. Review any misspelt words 3 times.

LOOK.   SAY.   COVER.   WRITE.   CHECK.

Practise

Practise 1

Practise 2

Practise 3

TIP Remember, look up each word in your dictionary to learn its meaning!

Need extra practise?
Printable blank practise sheet available from: www.lifelongeducation.com.au/spelling_practise_sheet
(also available on page 167)

Date: ....

Word List

ritual	dozen	deadly	branch	stove
quite	honour	nature	pose	think
boring	stress	strict	entity	butter

INSTRUCTIONS: Review the word list above and then cover. Have someone read out each word while you write them in the spaces below. Review any misspelt words 3 times.

LOOK.   SAY.   COVER.   WRITE.   CHECK.

Practise

Practise 1

Practise 2

Practise 3

TIP Remember, look up each word in your dictionary to learn its meaning!

Need extra practise?
Printable blank practise sheet available from: www.lifelongeducation.com.au/spelling_practise_sheet
(also available on page 167)

Date: ....

Word List

deck	ridge	shoe	super	river
dig	how	bride	high	follow
pause	engine	cookie	ban	aspect

INSTRUCTIONS: Review the word list above and then cover. Have someone read out each word while you write them in the spaces below. Review any misspelt words 3 times.

LOOK.   SAY.   COVER.   WRITE.   CHECK.

Practise

Practise 1

Practise 2

Practise 3

TIP Remember, look up each word in your dictionary to learn its meaning!

Need extra practise?
Printable blank practise sheet available from: www.lifelongeducation.com.au/spelling_practise_sheet
(also available on page 167)

SET 75

Word List

into	slope	odd	nose	bus
God	bow	bat	many	jungle
bike	story	cabin	our	sieve

INSTRUCTIONS: Review the word list above and then cover. Have someone read out each word while you write them in the spaces below. Review any misspelt words 3 times.

LOOK.   SAY.   COVER.   WRITE.   CHECK.

Practise

Practise 1

Practise 2

Practise 3

TIP Remember, look up each word in your dictionary to learn its meaning!

Need extra practise?
Printable blank practise sheet available from: www.lifelongeducation.com.au/spelling_practise_sheet
(also available on page 167)

Date: ....

Word List

where	**strip**	**smoke**	**file**	**cargo**
insect	**ignore**	**flee**	**use**	**row**
shout	**ours**	**idea**	**praise**	**crash**

INSTRUCTIONS: Review the word list above and then cover. Have someone read out each word while you write them in the spaces below. Review any misspelt words 3 times.

LOOK. SAY. COVER. WRITE. CHECK.

Practise

Practise 1

Practise 2

Practise 3

TIP Remember, look up each word in your dictionary to learn its meaning!

Need extra practise?
Printable blank practise sheet available from: www.lifelongeducation.com.au/spelling_practise_sheet
(also available on page 167)

SET 77

Word List

hence	seem	dad	prove	zone
good	bless	active	lay	given
gear	borrow	formal	minor	slap

INSTRUCTIONS: Review the word list above and then cover. Have someone read out each word while you write them in the spaces below. Review any misspelt words 3 times.

LOOK.   SAY.   COVER.   WRITE.   CHECK.

Practise

Practise 1

Practise 2

Practise 3

TIP — Remember, look up each word in your dictionary to learn its meaning!

Need extra practise?
Printable blank practise sheet available from: www.lifelongeducation.com.au/spelling_practise_sheet
(also available on page 167)

Date: ....

Word List

body	museum	triple	career	will
league	kick	onion	owner	neat
human	closer	disk	thigh	rack

INSTRUCTIONS: Review the word list above and then cover. Have someone read out each word while you write them in the spaces below. Review any misspelt words 3 times.

LOOK.   SAY.   COVER.   WRITE.   CHECK.

Practise

Practise 1

Practise 2

Practise 3

TIP Remember, look up each word in your dictionary to learn its meaning!

Need extra practise?
Printable blank practise sheet available from: www.lifelongeducation.com.au/spelling_practise_sheet
(also available on page 167)

Date: ....

Word List

twelve	club	handle	finish	toss
few	pistol	drop	cage	dried
jaw	height	blame	knead	oblige

INSTRUCTIONS: Review the word list above and then cover. Have someone read out each word while you write them in the spaces below. Review any misspelt words 3 times.

LOOK.   SAY.   COVER.   WRITE.   CHECK.

Practise

Practise 1

Practise 2

Practise 3

TIP Remember, look up each word in your dictionary to learn its meaning!

Need extra practise?
Printable blank practise sheet available from: www.lifelongeducation.com.au/spelling_practise_sheet
(also available on page 167)

SET 80

Word List

cause	tie	more	snake	stair
animal	share	among	clock	lend
strain	due	fewer	sole	guilt

INSTRUCTIONS: Review the word list above and then cover. Have someone read out each word while you write them in the spaces below. Review any misspelt words 3 times.

LOOK.   SAY.   COVER.   WRITE.   CHECK.

Practise

Practise 1

Practise 2

Practise 3

TIP Remember, look up each word in your dictionary to learn its meaning!

Need extra practise?
Printable blank practise sheet available from: www.lifelongeducation.com.au/spelling_practise_sheet
(also available on page 167)

Date: ....

Word List

who	**sweet**	**dough**	**ahead**	**realm**
happen	**tooth**	**waist**	**ledge**	**owe**
tea	**chest**	**video**	**hay**	**able**

INSTRUCTIONS: Review the word list above and then cover. Have someone read out each word while you write them in the spaces below. Review any misspelt words 3 times.

LOOK.   SAY.   COVER.   WRITE.   CHECK.

Practise

Practise 1

Practise 2

Practise 3

TIP Remember, look up each word in your dictionary to learn its meaning!

Need extra practise?
Printable blank practise sheet available from: www.lifelongeducation.com.au/spelling_practise_sheet
(also available on page 167)

SET 82

Word List

award	trace	plea	vanish	belong
across	half	glad	cold	star
upset	the	big	new	banker

INSTRUCTIONS: Review the word list above and then cover. Have someone read out each word while you write them in the spaces below. Review any misspelt words 3 times.

LOOK.   SAY.   COVER.   WRITE.   CHECK.

Practise

Practise 1

Practise 2

Practise 3

TIP Remember, look up each word in your dictionary to learn its meaning!

Need extra practise?
Printable blank practise sheet available from: www.lifelongeducation.com.au/spelling_practise_sheet
(also available on page 167)

SET 83

Date: ....

Word List

hunter	stage	fierce	steam	behind
three	party	best	access	fuel
fit	box	quote	night	modern

INSTRUCTIONS: Review the word list above and then cover. Have someone read out each word while you write them in the spaces below. Review any misspelt words 3 times.

LOOK.   SAY.   COVER.   WRITE.   CHECK.

Practise

Practise 1

Practise 2

Practise 3

TIP Remember, look up each word in your dictionary to learn its meaning!

Need extra practise?
Printable blank practise sheet available from: www.lifelongeducation.com.au/spelling_practise_sheet
(also available on page 167)

The Ultimate Spelling List (Book 1): Most Common and Important Spoken and Written Words in English

SET 84

Word List

trial	sector	writer	cheat	aside
nation	remind	bird	marker	juror
court	item	scared	pound	brief

INSTRUCTIONS: Review the word list above and then cover. Have someone read out each word while you write them in the spaces below. Review any misspelt words 3 times.

LOOK.　SAY.　COVER.　WRITE.　CHECK.

Practise

Practise 1

Practise 2

Practise 3

TIP　Remember, look up each word in your dictionary to learn its meaning!

Need extra practise?
Printable blank practise sheet available from: www.lifelongeducation.com.au/spelling_practise_sheet
(also available on page 167)

SET 85

Date: ....

Word List

lobby	gym	sake	tactic	second
myself	evil	unique	main	bear
almost	fool	thrive	cloth	maybe

INSTRUCTIONS: Review the word list above and then cover. Have someone read out each word while you write them in the spaces below. Review any misspelt words 3 times.

LOOK.   SAY.   COVER.   WRITE.   CHECK.

Practise

Practise 1

Practise 2

Practise 3

TIP Remember, look up each word in your dictionary to learn its meaning!

Need extra practise?
Printable blank practise sheet available from: www.lifelongeducation.com.au/spelling_practise_sheet
(also available on page 167)

The Ultimate Spelling List (Book 1): Most Common and Important Spoken and Written Words in English

SET 86

Word List

cable	cave	desk	fight	lost
strike	skull	cup	assign	call
pig	add	dancer	reason	wind

INSTRUCTIONS: Review the word list above and then cover. Have someone read out each word while you write them in the spaces below. Review any misspelt words 3 times.

LOOK.   SAY.   COVER.   WRITE.   CHECK.

Practise

Practise 1

Practise 2

Practise 3

TIP Remember, look up each word in your dictionary to learn its meaning!

Need extra practise?
Printable blank practise sheet available from: www.lifelongeducation.com.au/spelling_practise_sheet
(also available on page 167)

Date: ....

Word List

run	defend	mentor	rival	exam
teach	partly	tend	tip	hungry
clue	sodium	cancel	own	sofa

INSTRUCTIONS: Review the word list above and then cover. Have someone read out each word while you write them in the spaces below. Review any misspelt words 3 times.

LOOK.   SAY.   COVER.   WRITE.   CHECK.

Practise

Practise 1

Practise 2

Practise 3

TIP > Remember, look up each word in your dictionary to learn its meaning!

Need extra practise?
Printable blank practise sheet available from: www.lifelongeducation.com.au/spelling_practise_sheet
(also available on page 167)

SET 88

Word List

plot	expand	wage	see	common
pole	silent	cling	roof	fan
assess	civil	aim	cruise	mainly

INSTRUCTIONS: Review the word list above and then cover. Have someone read out each word while you write them in the spaces below. Review any misspelt words 3 times.

LOOK.   SAY.   COVER.   WRITE.   CHECK.

Practise

Practise 1

Practise 2

Practise 3

TIP Remember, look up each word in your dictionary to learn its meaning!

Need extra practise?
Printable blank practise sheet available from: www.lifelongeducation.com.au/spelling_practise_sheet
(also available on page 167)

Date: ....

Word List

drift	soon	enter	hate	okay
unit	press	soccer	hello	rifle
allow	campus	happy	liver	ballot

INSTRUCTIONS: Review the word list above and then cover. Have someone read out each word while you write them in the spaces below. Review any misspelt words 3 times.

LOOK.   SAY.   COVER.   WRITE.   CHECK.

Practise

Practise 1

Practise 2

Practise 3

TIP Remember, look up each word in your dictionary to learn its meaning!

Need extra practise?
Printable blank practise sheet available from: www.lifelongeducation.com.au/spelling_practise_sheet
(also available on page 167)

SET 90

Word List

task	nine	marry	secret	daily
have	narrow	after	attach	bay
frown	pilot	mother	yours	wooden

INSTRUCTIONS: Review the word list above and then cover. Have someone read out each word while you write them in the spaces below. Review any misspelt words 3 times.

LOOK.   SAY.   COVER.   WRITE.   CHECK.

Practise

Practise 1

Practise 2

Practise 3

TIP Remember, look up each word in your dictionary to learn its meaning!

Need extra practise?
Printable blank practise sheet available from: www.lifelongeducation.com.au/spelling_practise_sheet
(also available on page 167)

Date: ....

Word List

goal	aide	each	nasty	smell
answer	toe	badly	only	news
trap	statue	free	open	shoot

INSTRUCTIONS: Review the word list above and then cover. Have someone read out each word while you write them in the spaces below. Review any misspelt words 3 times.

LOOK.   SAY.   COVER.   WRITE.   CHECK.

Practise

Practise 1

Practise 2

Practise 3

TIP Remember, look up each word in your dictionary to learn its meaning!

Need extra practise?
Printable blank practise sheet available from: www.lifelongeducation.com.au/spelling_practise_sheet
(also available on page 167)

SET 92

Date: ....

Word List

weave	meat	act	recipe	hunt
score	deer	green	bother	stake
proper	hall	this	copy	edit

INSTRUCTIONS: Review the word list above and then cover. Have someone read out each word while you write them in the spaces below. Review any misspelt words 3 times.

LOOK.   SAY.   COVER.   WRITE.   CHECK.

Practise

Practise 1

Practise 2

Practise 3

(TIP) Remember, look up each word in your dictionary to learn its meaning!

Need extra practise?
Printable blank practise sheet available from: www.lifelongeducation.com.au/spelling_practise_sheet
(also available on page 167)

SET 93

Date: ....

Word List

resign	convey	pastor	resign	convey
pastor	two	muscle	jump	south
needle	guess	fraud	hole	magic

INSTRUCTIONS: Review the word list above and then cover. Have someone read out each word while you write them in the spaces below. Review any misspelt words 3 times.

LOOK.   SAY.   COVER.   WRITE.   CHECK.

Practise

Practise 1

Practise 2

Practise 3

TIP Remember, look up each word in your dictionary to learn its meaning!

Need extra practise?
Printable blank practise sheet available from: www.lifelongeducation.com.au/spelling_practise_sheet
(also available on page 167)

The Ultimate Spelling List (Book 1): Most Common and Important Spoken and Written Words in English

SET 94

Word List

empty	fill	shift	gene	oak
limp	shake	sight	verbal	May
bake	cord	none	pure	mad

INSTRUCTIONS: Review the word list above and then cover. Have someone read out each word while you write them in the spaces below. Review any misspelt words 3 times.

LOOK. SAY. COVER. WRITE. CHECK.

Practise

Practise 1

Practise 2

Practise 3

TIP ⬡ Remember, look up each word in your dictionary to learn its meaning!

Need extra practise?
Printable blank practise sheet available from: www.lifelongeducation.com.au/spelling_practise_sheet
(also available on page 167)

SET 95

Word List

arise	core	array	spot	during
fact	skin	choose	suit	pull
canvas	reform	parish	record	there

INSTRUCTIONS: Review the word list above and then cover. Have someone read out each word while you write them in the spaces below. Review any misspelt words 3 times.

LOOK.   SAY.   COVER.   WRITE.   CHECK.

Practise

Practise 1

Practise 2

Practise 3

TIP Remember, look up each word in your dictionary to learn its meaning!

Need extra practise?
Printable blank practise sheet available from: www.lifelongeducation.com.au/spelling_practise_sheet
(also available on page 167)

Date: ....

Word List

thumb	rope	cheese	drive	highly
review	learn	urge	enjoy	policy
then	fire	minute	spread	atop

INSTRUCTIONS: Review the word list above and then cover. Have someone read out each word while you write them in the spaces below. Review any misspelt words 3 times.

LOOK.   SAY.   COVER.   WRITE.   CHECK.

Practise

Practise 1

Practise 2

Practise 3

TIP Remember, look up each word in your dictionary to learn its meaning!

Need extra practise?
Printable blank practise sheet available from: www.lifelongeducation.com.au/spelling_practise_sheet
(also available on page 167)

SET 97

Word List

adult	artist	shade	safe	pant
found	child	slide	push	fail
pump	wheat	ring	fruit	deploy

INSTRUCTIONS: Review the word list above and then cover. Have someone read out each word while you write them in the spaces below. Review any misspelt words 3 times.

LOOK.   SAY.   COVER.   WRITE.   CHECK.

Practise

Practise 1

Practise 2

Practise 3

TIP Remember, look up each word in your dictionary to learn its meaning!

Need extra practise?
Printable blank practise sheet available from: www.lifelongeducation.com.au/spelling_practise_sheet
(also available on page 167)

SET 98

Word List

third	chance	nice	flash	nut
judge	grace	mouse	studio	web
pitch	mate	fast	load	beam

INSTRUCTIONS: Review the word list above and then cover. Have someone read out each word while you write them in the spaces below. Review any misspelt words 3 times.

LOOK.   SAY.   COVER.   WRITE.   CHECK.

Practise

Practise 1

Practise 2

Practise 3

TIP Remember, look up each word in your dictionary to learn its meaning!

Need extra practise?
Printable blank practise sheet available from: www.lifelongeducation.com.au/spelling_practise_sheet
(also available on page 167)

SET 99

Word List

expert	**salad**	**show**	**trim**	**bind**
doubt	**rear**	**love**	**motor**	**skirt**
glory	**really**	**toward**	**staff**	**rather**

INSTRUCTIONS: Review the word list above and then cover. Have someone read out each word while you write them in the spaces below. Review any misspelt words 3 times.

LOOK.   SAY.   COVER.   WRITE.   CHECK.

Practise

Practise 1

Practise 2

Practise 3

TIP Remember, look up each word in your dictionary to learn its meaning!

Need extra practise?
Printable blank practise sheet available from: www.lifelongeducation.com.au/spelling_practise_sheet
(also available on page 167)

SET 100

Word List

outfit	soften	novel	eight	nerve
truck	term	gas	event	bone
faint	hold	acid	his	diet

INSTRUCTIONS: Review the word list above and then cover. Have someone read out each word while you write them in the spaces below. Review any misspelt words 3 times.

LOOK. SAY. COVER. WRITE. CHECK.

Practise

Practise 1

Practise 2

Practise 3

TIP Remember, look up each word in your dictionary to learn its meaning!

Need extra practise?
Printable blank practise sheet available from: www.lifelongeducation.com.au/spelling_practise_sheet
(also available on page 167)

SET 101

Date: ....

Word List

turkey	scare	host	debut	solar
plenty	valid	folk	safely	focus
solid	spell	thread	future	plant

INSTRUCTIONS: Review the word list above and then cover. Have someone read out each word while you write them in the spaces below. Review any misspelt words 3 times.

LOOK.　SAY.　COVER.　WRITE.　CHECK.

Practise

Practise 1

Practise 2

Practise 3

TIP Remember, look up each word in your dictionary to learn its meaning!

Need extra practise?
Printable blank practise sheet available from: www.lifelongeducation.com.au/spelling_practise_sheet
(also available on page 167)

The Ultimate Spelling List (Book 1): Most Common and Important Spoken and Written Words in English

SET 102

Word List

shorts	streak	head	versus	above
bet	differ	ill	boat	slave
wonder	bright	label	escape	couple

INSTRUCTIONS: Review the word list above and then cover. Have someone read out each word while you write them in the spaces below. Review any misspelt words 3 times.

LOOK.   SAY.   COVER.   WRITE.   CHECK.

Practise

Practise 1

Practise 2

Practise 3

TIP Remember, look up each word in your dictionary to learn its meaning!

Need extra practise?
Printable blank practise sheet available from: www.lifelongeducation.com.au/spelling_practise_sheet
(also available on page 167)

SET 103

Word List

invite	reader	cry	earth	lemon
now	deputy	assert	bury	text
give	unless	global	script	relate

INSTRUCTIONS: Review the word list above and then cover. Have someone read out each word while you write them in the spaces below. Review any misspelt words 3 times.

LOOK.   SAY.   COVER.   WRITE.   CHECK.

Practise

Practise 1

Practise 2

Practise 3

TIP — Remember, look up each word in your dictionary to learn its meaning!

Need extra practise?
Printable blank practise sheet available from: www.lifelongeducation.com.au/spelling_practise_sheet
(also available on page 167)

SET 104

Word List

twin	cruel	galaxy	burst	supply
laugh	slice	time	sheer	robot
fair	when	bench	feed	low

INSTRUCTIONS: Review the word list above and then cover. Have someone read out each word while you write them in the spaces below. Review any misspelt words 3 times.

LOOK.   SAY.   COVER.   WRITE.   CHECK.

Practise

Practise 1

Practise 2

Practise 3

TIP Remember, look up each word in your dictionary to learn its meaning!

Need extra practise?
Printable blank practise sheet available from: www.lifelongeducation.com.au/spelling_practise_sheet
(also available on page 167)

SET 105

Word List

horse	**store**	**mere**	**camp**	**chin**
vocal	**brave**	**flag**	**spouse**	**tennis**
mayor	**end**	**log**	**origin**	**ruin**

INSTRUCTIONS: Review the word list above and then cover. Have someone read out each word while you write them in the spaces below. Review any misspelt words 3 times.

LOOK.   SAY.   COVER.   WRITE.   CHECK.

Practise

Practise 1

Practise 2

Practise 3

TIP Remember, look up each word in your dictionary to learn its meaning!

Need extra practise?
Printable blank practise sheet available from: www.lifelongeducation.com.au/spelling_practise_sheet
(also available on page 167)

SET 106

Word List

scarf	pickup	slip	loop	port
next	remove	start	elite	sweat
mutter	duty	harm	under	would

INSTRUCTIONS: Review the word list above and then cover. Have someone read out each word while you write them in the spaces below. Review any misspelt words 3 times.

LOOK.   SAY.   COVER.   WRITE.   CHECK.

Practise

Practise 1

Practise 2

Practise 3

TIP Remember, look up each word in your dictionary to learn its meaning!

Need extra practise?
Printable blank practise sheet available from: www.lifelongeducation.com.au/spelling_practise_sheet
(also available on page 167)

SET 107

Date: ....

Word List

pretty	broken	off	admire	sphere
leader	suffer	bean	comply	which
sure	stock	rarely	find	faith

INSTRUCTIONS: Review the word list above and then cover. Have someone read out each word while you write them in the spaces below. Review any misspelt words 3 times.

LOOK.   SAY.   COVER.   WRITE.   CHECK.

Practise

Practise 1

Practise 2

Practise 3

TIP Remember, look up each word in your dictionary to learn its meaning!

Need extra practise?
Printable blank practise sheet available from: www.lifelongeducation.com.au/spelling_practise_sheet
(also available on page 167)

The Ultimate Spelling List (Book 1): Most Common and Important Spoken and Written Words in English

SET 108

Date: ....

Word List

blind	barn	bed	top	face
emerge	son	hunger	widely	essay
screen	export	pork	warmth	arm

INSTRUCTIONS: Review the word list above and then cover. Have someone read out each word while you write them in the spaces below. Review any misspelt words 3 times.

LOOK.   SAY.   COVER.   WRITE.   CHECK.

Practise

Practise 1

Practise 2

Practise 3

TIP Remember, look up each word in your dictionary to learn its meaning!

Need extra practise?
Printable blank practise sheet available from: www.lifelongeducation.com.au/spelling_practise_sheet
(also available on page 167)

The Ultimate Spelling List (Book 1): Most Common and Important Spoken and Written Words in English

Date: ....

Word List

noise	report	rely	fairly	ship
energy	resume	blink	back	manual
useful	coffee	mass	busy	phase

INSTRUCTIONS: Review the word list above and then cover. Have someone read out each word while you write them in the spaces below. Review any misspelt words 3 times.

LOOK.   SAY.   COVER.   WRITE.   CHECK.

Practise

Practise 1

Practise 2

Practise 3

(TIP) Remember, look up each word in your dictionary to learn its meaning!

Need extra practise?
Printable blank practise sheet available from: www.lifelongeducation.com.au/spelling_practise_sheet
(also available on page 167)

SET 110

Date: ....

Word List

demand	carbon	mobile	air	wander
clay	March	thing	pray	water
via	van	enough	bid	swing

INSTRUCTIONS: Review the word list above and then cover. Have someone read out each word while you write them in the spaces below. Review any misspelt words 3 times.

LOOK.   SAY.   COVER.   WRITE.   CHECK.

Practise

Practise 1

Practise 2

Practise 3

TIP Remember, look up each word in your dictionary to learn its meaning!

Need extra practise?
Printable blank practise sheet available from: www.lifelongeducation.com.au/spelling_practise_sheet
(also available on page 167)

The Ultimate Spelling List (Book 1): Most Common and Important Spoken and Written Words in English

115

SET 111

Word List

depth	twenty	nobody	she	path
palace	puzzle	oppose	plus	coat
all	prefer	effect	fresh	riot

INSTRUCTIONS: Review the word list above and then cover. Have someone read out each word while you write them in the spaces below. Review any misspelt words 3 times.

LOOK.   SAY.   COVER.   WRITE.   CHECK.

Practise

Practise 1

Practise 2

Practise 3

TIP Remember, look up each word in your dictionary to learn its meaning!

Need extra practise?
Printable blank practise sheet available from: www.lifelongeducation.com.au/spelling_practise_sheet
(also available on page 167)

SET 112

Word List

string	wine	field	bring	try
filter	pile	mixed	immune	fog
lens	bare	bee	April	liquid

INSTRUCTIONS: Review the word list above and then cover. Have someone read out each word while you write them in the spaces below. Review any misspelt words 3 times.

LOOK.   SAY.   COVER.   WRITE.   CHECK.

Practise

Practise 1

Practise 2

Practise 3

TIP Remember, look up each word in your dictionary to learn its meaning!

Need extra practise?
Printable blank practise sheet available from: www.lifelongeducation.com.au/spelling_practise_sheet
(also available on page 167)

SET 113

Word List

flow	desire	combat	media	column
shadow	modify	deeply	figure	poor
soak	truly	rail	lawn	large

INSTRUCTIONS: Review the word list above and then cover. Have someone read out each word while you write them in the spaces below. Review any misspelt words 3 times.

LOOK.   SAY.   COVER.   WRITE.   CHECK.

Practise

Practise 1

Practise 2

Practise 3

TIP Remember, look up each word in your dictionary to learn its meaning!

Need extra practise?
Printable blank practise sheet available from: www.lifelongeducation.com.au/spelling_practise_sheet
(also available on page 167)

SET 114

Word List

deem	list	race	nearly	awful
leaf	chew	cattle	forum	swim
red	bronze	hurry	angle	simply

INSTRUCTIONS: Review the word list above and then cover. Have someone read out each word while you write them in the spaces below. Review any misspelt words 3 times.

LOOK.   SAY.   COVER.   WRITE.   CHECK.

Practise

Practise 1

Practise 2

Practise 3

TIP Remember, look up each word in your dictionary to learn its meaning!

Need extra practise?
Printable blank practise sheet available from: www.lifelongeducation.com.au/spelling_practise_sheet
(also available on page 167)

SET 115

Word List

change	injure	scene	west	flame
frame	here	scary	send	reward
regard	diary	rib	runner	wave

INSTRUCTIONS: Review the word list above and then cover. Have someone read out each word while you write them in the spaces below. Review any misspelt words 3 times.

LOOK. SAY. COVER. WRITE. CHECK.

Practise

Practise 1

Practise 2

Practise 3

TIP Remember, look up each word in your dictionary to learn its meaning!

Need extra practise?
Printable blank practise sheet available from: www.lifelongeducation.com.au/spelling_practise_sheet
(also available on page 167)

SET 116

Word List

either	master	mail	rider	seldom
risk	track	author	peace	kneel
lack	stem	divine	eighth	count

INSTRUCTIONS: Review the word list above and then cover. Have someone read out each word while you write them in the spaces below. Review any misspelt words 3 times.

LOOK.   SAY.   COVER.   WRITE.   CHECK.

Practise

Practise 1

Practise 2

Practise 3

TIP Remember, look up each word in your dictionary to learn its meaning!

Need extra practise?
Printable blank practise sheet available from: www.lifelongeducation.com.au/spelling_practise_sheet
(also available on page 167)

SET 117

Word List

spray	damage	equal	timber	kettle
lunch	virus	shed	grape	debate
wake	brush	nearby	fry	ago

INSTRUCTIONS: Review the word list above and then cover. Have someone read out each word while you write them in the spaces below. Review any misspelt words 3 times.

LOOK.   SAY.   COVER.   WRITE.   CHECK.

Practise

Practise 1

Practise 2

Practise 3

TIP Remember, look up each word in your dictionary to learn its meaning!

Need extra practise?
Printable blank practise sheet available from: www.lifelongeducation.com.au/spelling_practise_sheet
(also available on page 167)

SET 118

Word List

tight	iron	chart	native	trash
golf	tent	sneer	clay	steak
other	earn	skill	depend	extent

INSTRUCTIONS: Review the word list above and then cover. Have someone read out each word while you write them in the spaces below. Review any misspelt words 3 times.

LOOK.   SAY.   COVER.   WRITE.   CHECK.

Practise

Practise 1

Practise 2

Practise 3

TIP Remember, look up each word in your dictionary to learn its meaning!

Need extra practise?
Printable blank practise sheet available from: www.lifelongeducation.com.au/spelling_practise_sheet
(also available on page 167)

SET 119

Word List

mirror	eager	worry	permit	player
coup	severe	law	flying	tiny
gun	abroad	watch	grade	safety

INSTRUCTIONS: Review the word list above and then cover. Have someone read out each word while you write them in the spaces below. Review any misspelt words 3 times.

LOOK.   SAY.   COVER.   WRITE.   CHECK.

Practise

Practise 1

Practise 2

Practise 3

TIP Remember, look up each word in your dictionary to learn its meaning!

Need extra practise?
Printable blank practise sheet available from: www.lifelongeducation.com.au/spelling_practise_sheet
(also available on page 167)

SET 120

Word List

bite	clerk	elder	point	save
mean	sing	skip	corn	obtain
vary	job	some	castle	retire

INSTRUCTIONS: Review the word list above and then cover. Have someone read out each word while you write them in the spaces below. Review any misspelt words 3 times.

LOOK.   SAY.   COVER.   WRITE.   CHECK.

Practise

Practise 1

Practise 2

Practise 3

TIP Remember, look up each word in your dictionary to learn its meaning!

Need extra practise?
Printable blank practise sheet available from: www.lifelongeducation.com.au/spelling_practise_sheet
(also available on page 167)

Date: ....

Word List

attend	shot	burn	sensor	again
five	desert	pencil	cow	fixed
fun	towel	name	birth	motion

INSTRUCTIONS: Review the word list above and then cover. Have someone read out each word while you write them in the spaces below. Review any misspelt words 3 times.

LOOK.   SAY.   COVER.   WRITE.   CHECK.

Practise

Practise 1

Practise 2

Practise 3

TIP Remember, look up each word in your dictionary to learn its meaning!

Need extra practise?
Printable blank practise sheet available from: www.lifelongeducation.com.au/spelling_practise_sheet
(also available on page 167)

Date: ....

Word List

inner	peak	hire	goat	very
terror	chill	size	turn	define
spoon	sheep	bad	long	claim

INSTRUCTIONS: Review the word list above and then cover. Have someone read out each word while you write them in the spaces below. Review any misspelt words 3 times.

LOOK.   SAY.   COVER.   WRITE.   CHECK.

Practise

Practise 1

Practise 2

Practise 3

TIP Remember, look up each word in your dictionary to learn its meaning!

Need extra practise?
Printable blank practise sheet available from: www.lifelongeducation.com.au/spelling_practise_sheet
(also available on page 167)

SET 123

Date: ....

Word List

poet	throw	speed	image	along
much	genre	visual	gifted	plane
soar	course	rim	room	lawyer

INSTRUCTIONS: Review the word list above and then cover. Have someone read out each word while you write them in the spaces below. Review any misspelt words 3 times.

LOOK. SAY. COVER. WRITE. CHECK.

Practise

Practise 1

Practise 2

Practise 3

TIP Remember, look up each word in your dictionary to learn its meaning!

Need extra practise?
Printable blank practise sheet available from: www.lifelongeducation.com.au/spelling_practise_sheet
(also available on page 167)

The Ultimate Spelling List (Book 1): Most Common and Important Spoken and Written Words in English

SET 124

Date: ....

Word List

agenda	noon	for	plate	carrot
grab	banana	jar	sort	rub
expect	naval	park	data	cake

INSTRUCTIONS: Review the word list above and then cover. Have someone read out each word while you write them in the spaces below. Review any misspelt words 3 times.

LOOK.   SAY.   COVER.   WRITE.   CHECK.

Practise

Practise 1

Practise 2

Practise 3

TIP Remember, look up each word in your dictionary to learn its meaning!

Need extra practise?
Printable blank practise sheet available from: www.lifelongeducation.com.au/spelling_practise_sheet
(also available on page 167)

Date: ....

Word List

dense	**makeup**	**social**	**style**	**mental**
bloody	**blend**	**board**	**why**	**broad**
tunnel	**aunt**	**fly**	**get**	**globe**

INSTRUCTIONS: Review the word list above and then cover. Have someone read out each word while you write them in the spaces below. Review any misspelt words 3 times.

LOOK.   SAY.   COVER.   WRITE.   CHECK.

Practise

Practise 1

Practise 2

Practise 3

TIP Remember, look up each word in your dictionary to learn its meaning!

Need extra practise?
Printable blank practise sheet available from: www.lifelongeducation.com.au/spelling_practise_sheet
(also available on page 167)

Date: ....

Word List

note	though	toll	bar	thank
blade	cousin	ghost	serve	indeed
invade	exit	defeat	sauce	yellow

INSTRUCTIONS: Review the word list above and then cover. Have someone read out each word while you write them in the spaces below. Review any misspelt words 3 times.

LOOK. SAY. COVER. WRITE. CHECK.

Practise

Practise 1

Practise 2

Practise 3

TIP Remember, look up each word in your dictionary to learn its meaning!

Need extra practise?
Printable blank practise sheet available from: www.lifelongeducation.com.au/spelling_practise_sheet
(also available on page 167)

SET 127

Word List

salt	range	total	ticket	shower
employ	trait	order	normal	people
recent	reduce	fur	mode	fare

INSTRUCTIONS: Review the word list above and then cover. Have someone read out each word while you write them in the spaces below. Review any misspelt words 3 times.

LOOK.   SAY.   COVER.   WRITE.   CHECK.

Practise

Practise 1

Practise 2

Practise 3

TIP Remember, look up each word in your dictionary to learn its meaning!

Need extra practise?
Printable blank practise sheet available from: www.lifelongeducation.com.au/spelling_practise_sheet
(also available on page 167)

Date: ....

Word List

valley	**solely**	**help**	**nod**	**stack**
thin	**merit**	**grief**	**degree**	**sell**
spill	**hear**	**hug**	**rent**	**credit**

INSTRUCTIONS: Review the word list above and then cover. Have someone read out each word while you write them in the spaces below. Review any misspelt words 3 times.

LOOK.   SAY.   COVER.   WRITE.   CHECK.

Practise

Practise 1

Practise 2

Practise 3

TIP Remember, look up each word in your dictionary to learn its meaning!

Need extra practise?
Printable blank practise sheet available from: www.lifelongeducation.com.au/spelling_practise_sheet
(also available on page 167)

SET 129

Date: ....

Word List

office	rock	rip	last	tube
since	well	crime	enrol	weekly
motive	gaze	hazard	works	freely

INSTRUCTIONS: Review the word list above and then cover. Have someone read out each word while you write them in the spaces below. Review any misspelt words 3 times.

LOOK.   SAY.   COVER.   WRITE.   CHECK.

Practise

Practise 1

Practise 2

Practise 3

TIP Remember, look up each word in your dictionary to learn its meaning!

Need extra practise?
Printable blank practise sheet available from: www.lifelongeducation.com.au/spelling_practise_sheet
(also available on page 167)

SET 130

Word List

onto	refer	lot	speak	flip
light	too	train	imply	candle
hockey	bend	spin	ice	retain

INSTRUCTIONS: Review the word list above and then cover. Have someone read out each word while you write them in the spaces below. Review any misspelt words 3 times.

LOOK. SAY. COVER. WRITE. CHECK.

Practise

Practise 1

Practise 2

Practise 3

TIP Remember, look up each word in your dictionary to learn its meaning!

Need extra practise?
Printable blank practise sheet available from: www.lifelongeducation.com.au/spelling_practise_sheet
(also available on page 167)

SET 131

Word List

poem	form	choice	hotel	logic
entry	donate	injury	black	calm
mood	merely	search	finger	spy

INSTRUCTIONS: Review the word list above and then cover. Have someone read out each word while you write them in the spaces below. Review any misspelt words 3 times.

LOOK.   SAY.   COVER.   WRITE.   CHECK.

Practise

Practise 1

Practise 2

Practise 3

TIP Remember, look up each word in your dictionary to learn its meaning!

Need extra practise?
Printable blank practise sheet available from: www.lifelongeducation.com.au/spelling_practise_sheet
(also available on page 167)

SET 132

Word List

bridge	brutal	read	living	viewer
young	win	union	oxygen	manage
being	snow	dream	step	pin

INSTRUCTIONS: Review the word list above and then cover. Have someone read out each word while you write them in the spaces below. Review any misspelt words 3 times.

LOOK.   SAY.   COVER.   WRITE.   CHECK.

Practise

Practise 1

Practise 2

Practise 3

TIP Remember, look up each word in your dictionary to learn its meaning!

Need extra practise?
Printable blank practise sheet available from: www.lifelongeducation.com.au/spelling_practise_sheet
(also available on page 167)

SET 133

Word List

detail	limit	fabric	true	pasta
route	itself	bottom	bolt	leave
sit	direct	door	crazy	easy

INSTRUCTIONS: Review the word list above and then cover. Have someone read out each word while you write them in the spaces below. Review any misspelt words 3 times.

LOOK.   SAY.   COVER.   WRITE.   CHECK.

Practise

Practise 1

Practise 2

Practise 3

TIP Remember, look up each word in your dictionary to learn its meaning!

Need extra practise?
Printable blank practise sheet available from: www.lifelongeducation.com.au/spelling_practise_sheet
(also available on page 167)

SET 134

Word List

fix	nail	waste	stone	draw
tired	sleep	rescue	wealth	punch
cue	small	added	pride	divide

INSTRUCTIONS: Review the word list above and then cover. Have someone read out each word while you write them in the spaces below. Review any misspelt words 3 times.

LOOK.   SAY.   COVER.   WRITE.   CHECK.

Practise

Practise 1

Practise 2

Practise 3

TIP Remember, look up each word in your dictionary to learn its meaning!

Need extra practise?
Printable blank practise sheet available from: www.lifelongeducation.com.au/spelling_practise_sheet
(also available on page 167)

Date: ....

Word List

midst	movie	drag	harsh	colour
ski	cheek	should	commit	chunk
link	bucket	site	bold	stuff

INSTRUCTIONS: Review the word list above and then cover. Have someone read out each word while you write them in the spaces below. Review any misspelt words 3 times.

LOOK.   SAY.   COVER.   WRITE.   CHECK.

Practise

Practise 1

Practise 2

Practise 3

TIP Remember, look up each word in your dictionary to learn its meaning!

Need extra practise?
Printable blank practise sheet available from: www.lifelongeducation.com.au/spelling_practise_sheet
(also available on page 167)

SET 136

Word List

option	terms	abuse	shut	cream
cart	invest	fleet	notion	member
farmer	street	lap	hair	late

INSTRUCTIONS: Review the word list above and then cover. Have someone read out each word while you write them in the spaces below. Review any misspelt words 3 times.

LOOK. SAY. COVER. WRITE. CHECK.

Practise

Practise 1

Practise 2

Practise 3

TIP Remember, look up each word in your dictionary to learn its meaning!

Need extra practise?
Printable blank practise sheet available from: www.lifelongeducation.com.au/spelling_practise_sheet
(also available on page 167)

SET 137

Word List

series	tower	urban	purse	poetry
quiet	region	proof	old	male
helmet	cotton	game	winner	shrug

INSTRUCTIONS: Review the word list above and then cover. Have someone read out each word while you write them in the spaces below. Review any misspelt words 3 times.

LOOK.   SAY.   COVER.   WRITE.   CHECK.

Practise

Practise 1

Practise 2

Practise 3

TIP Remember, look up each word in your dictionary to learn its meaning!

Need extra practise?
Printable blank practise sheet available from: www.lifelongeducation.com.au/spelling_practise_sheet
(also available on page 167)

SET 138

Word List

song	close	stick	pie	basic
mostly	bulk	hide	agree	boast
sin	look	chase	sacred	sun

INSTRUCTIONS: Review the word list above and then cover. Have someone read out each word while you write them in the spaces below. Review any misspelt words 3 times.

LOOK.   SAY.   COVER.   WRITE.   CHECK.

Practise

Practise 1

Practise 2

Practise 3

TIP Remember, look up each word in your dictionary to learn its meaning!

Need extra practise?
Printable blank practise sheet available from: www.lifelongeducation.com.au/spelling_practise_sheet
(also available on page 167)

SET 139

Word List

tank	bond	grass	rebel	raw
music	unity	bit	both	gentle
alive	wash	button	equity	stroke

INSTRUCTIONS: Review the word list above and then cover. Have someone read out each word while you write them in the spaces below. Review any misspelt words 3 times.

LOOK.   SAY.   COVER.   WRITE.   CHECK.

Practise

Practise 1

Practise 2

Practise 3

TIP Remember, look up each word in your dictionary to learn its meaning!

Need extra practise?
Printable blank practise sheet available from: www.lifelongeducation.com.au/spelling_practise_sheet
(also available on page 167)

SET 140

Word List

school	shell	lid	root	milk
frozen	ethics	firm	weird	rank
brown	slight	joke	layer	trauma

INSTRUCTIONS: Review the word list above and then cover. Have someone read out each word while you write them in the spaces below. Review any misspelt words 3 times.

LOOK.   SAY.   COVER.   WRITE.   CHECK.

Practise

Practise 1

Practise 2

Practise 3

TIP Remember, look up each word in your dictionary to learn its meaning!

Need extra practise?
Printable blank practise sheet available from: www.lifelongeducation.com.au/spelling_practise_sheet
(also available on page 167)

SET 141

Word List

plead	cease	patron	block	but
behalf	photo	doll	click	softly
timing	week	base	assist	prayer

INSTRUCTIONS: Review the word list above and then cover. Have someone read out each word while you write them in the spaces below. Review any misspelt words 3 times.

LOOK.   SAY.   COVER.   WRITE.   CHECK.

Practise

Practise 1

Practise 2

Practise 3

(TIP) Remember, look up each word in your dictionary to learn its meaning!

Need extra practise?
Printable blank practise sheet available from: www.lifelongeducation.com.au/spelling_practise_sheet
(also available on page 167)

Date: ....

Word List

steer	wait	barrel	wrap	plain
land	chair	smile	rumor	advice
herb	pillow	trip	appeal	gap

INSTRUCTIONS: Review the word list above and then cover. Have someone read out each word while you write them in the spaces below. Review any misspelt words 3 times.

LOOK.   SAY.   COVER.   WRITE.   CHECK.

Practise

Practise 1

Practise 2

Practise 3

TIP Remember, look up each word in your dictionary to learn its meaning!

Need extra practise?
Printable blank practise sheet available from: www.lifelongeducation.com.au/spelling_practise_sheet
(also available on page 167)

SET 143

Word List

church	knock	these	clear	modest
tile	index	full	trend	offer
format	guy	laser	regime	youth

INSTRUCTIONS: Review the word list above and then cover. Have someone read out each word while you write them in the spaces below. Review any misspelt words 3 times.

LOOK.   SAY.   COVER.   WRITE.   CHECK.

Practise

Practise 1

Practise 2

Practise 3

TIP Remember, look up each word in your dictionary to learn its meaning!

Need extra practise?
Printable blank practise sheet available from: www.lifelongeducation.com.au/spelling_practise_sheet
(also available on page 167)

SET 144

Word List

barely	sister	dump	pipe	wise
thick	elbow	hook	newly	risky
sales	cover	could	tall	upper

INSTRUCTIONS: Review the word list above and then cover. Have someone read out each word while you write them in the spaces below. Review any misspelt words 3 times.

LOOK.   SAY.   COVER.   WRITE.   CHECK.

Practise

Practise 1

Practise 2

Practise 3

TIP Remember, look up each word in your dictionary to learn its meaning!

Need extra practise?
Printable blank practise sheet available from: www.lifelongeducation.com.au/spelling_practise_sheet
(also available on page 167)

SET 145

Word List

crawl	asleep	cool	threat	manner
early	symbol	fever	soft	occur
decent	shape	exceed	toy	first

INSTRUCTIONS: Review the word list above and then cover. Have someone read out each word while you write them in the spaces below. Review any misspelt words 3 times.

LOOK.   SAY.   COVER.   WRITE.   CHECK.

Practise

Practise 1

Practise 2

Practise 3

TIP Remember, look up each word in your dictionary to learn its meaning!

Need extra practise?
Printable blank practise sheet available from: www.lifelongeducation.com.au/spelling_practise_sheet
(also available on page 167)

SET 146

Word List

fetch	ward	sore	rude	tablet
racing	dull	plug	autumn	lick
lounge	taxi	lamb	granny	windy

INSTRUCTIONS: Review the word list above and then cover. Have someone read out each word while you write them in the spaces below. Review any misspelt words 3 times.

LOOK.   SAY.   COVER.   WRITE.   CHECK.

Practise

Practise 1

Practise 2

Practise 3

TIP Remember, look up each word in your dictionary to learn its meaning!

Need extra practise?
Printable blank practise sheet available from: www.lifelongeducation.com.au/spelling_practise_sheet
(also available on page 167)

SET 147

Word List

pupil	jumper	dollar	shave	bang
nicely	supper	mum	sew	holder
cereal	handy	tidy	reckon	heater

INSTRUCTIONS: Review the word list above and then cover. Have someone read out each word while you write them in the spaces below. Review any misspelt words 3 times.

LOOK.   SAY.   COVER.   WRITE.   CHECK.

Practise

Practise 1

Practise 2

Practise 3

TIP Remember, look up each word in your dictionary to learn its meaning!

Need extra practise?
Printable blank practise sheet available from: www.lifelongeducation.com.au/spelling_practise_sheet
(also available on page 167)

SET 148

Word List

wool	boiler	starve	become	pardon
email	pity	steal	stamp	parcel
cinema	tin	prince	filthy	spoil

INSTRUCTIONS: Review the word list above and then cover. Have someone read out each word while you write them in the spaces below. Review any misspelt words 3 times.

LOOK.   SAY.   COVER.   WRITE.   CHECK.

Practise

Practise 1

Practise 2

Practise 3

TIP Remember, look up each word in your dictionary to learn its meaning!

Need extra practise?
Printable blank practise sheet available from: www.lifelongeducation.com.au/spelling_practise_sheet
(also available on page 167)

SET 149

Date: ....

Word List

bacon	bound	lazy	clever	messy
vet	polite	stall	fulfil	petrol
slim	fancy	deaf	gram	crown

INSTRUCTIONS: Review the word list above and then cover. Have someone read out each word while you write them in the spaces below. Review any misspelt words 3 times.

LOOK.   SAY.   COVER.   WRITE.   CHECK.

Practise

Practise 1

Practise 2

Practise 3

TIP Remember, look up each word in your dictionary to learn its meaning!

Need extra practise?
Printable blank practise sheet available from: www.lifelongeducation.com.au/spelling_practise_sheet
(also available on page 167)

Date: ....

Word List

colour	maths	bin	lump	bored
means	lad	tyre	noisy	pint
cent	chap	theirs	mile	bump

INSTRUCTIONS: Review the word list above and then cover. Have someone read out each word while you write them in the spaces below. Review any misspelt words 3 times.

LOOK.   SAY.   COVER.   WRITE.   CHECK.

Practise

Practise 1

Practise 2

Practise 3

TIP Remember, look up each word in your dictionary to learn its meaning!

Need extra practise?
Printable blank practise sheet available from: www.lifelongeducation.com.au/spelling_practise_sheet
(also available on page 167)

Date: ....

Word List

keen	worse	bye	cheque	toast
jam	lively	wicked	goods	lord
vague	loaf	graph	fridge	queue

INSTRUCTIONS: Review the word list above and then cover. Have someone read out each word while you write them in the spaces below. Review any misspelt words 3 times.

LOOK.   SAY.   COVER.   WRITE.   CHECK.

Practise

Practise 1

Practise 2

Practise 3

TIP Remember, look up each word in your dictionary to learn its meaning!

Need extra practise?
Printable blank practise sheet available from: www.lifelongeducation.com.au/spelling_practise_sheet
(also available on page 167)

SET 152

Word List

grey	fuss	madam	purely	pants
packet	urgent	inch	swap	tricky
cherry	united	chat	daft	rob

INSTRUCTIONS: Review the word list above and then cover. Have someone read out each word while you write them in the spaces below. Review any misspelt words 3 times.

LOOK.   SAY.   COVER.   WRITE.   CHECK.

Practise

Practise 1

Practise 2

Practise 3

TIP Remember, look up each word in your dictionary to learn its meaning!

Need extra practise?
Printable blank practise sheet available from: www.lifelongeducation.com.au/spelling_practise_sheet
(also available on page 167)

SET 153

Date: ....

Word List

blew	came	cane	chat	claw
crown	cube	dew	fell	flew
fry	gave	going	gone	grew

INSTRUCTIONS: Review the word list above and then cover. Have someone read out each word while you write them in the spaces below. Review any misspelt words 3 times.

LOOK.   SAY.   COVER.   WRITE.   CHECK.

Practise

Practise 1

Practise 2

Practise 3

TIP Remember, look up each word in your dictionary to learn its meaning!

Need extra practise?
Printable blank practise sheet available from: www.lifelongeducation.com.au/spelling_practise_sheet
(also available on page 167)

SET 154

Word List

kite	maid	men	mice	mint
sank	snore	sold	took	broom
bead	does	drip	flaw	flap

INSTRUCTIONS: Review the word list above and then cover. Have someone read out each word while you write them in the spaces below. Review any misspelt words 3 times.

LOOK.   SAY.   COVER.   WRITE.   CHECK.

Practise

Practise 1

Practise 2

Practise 3

TIP Remember, look up each word in your dictionary to learn its meaning!

Need extra practise?
Printable blank practise sheet available from: www.lifelongeducation.com.au/spelling_practise_sheet
(also available on page 167)

SET 155

Word List

flake	canal	goes	lump	rake
rust	said	says	spoke	stain
stamp	stood	stuck	toast	went

INSTRUCTIONS: Review the word list above and then cover. Have someone read out each word while you write them in the spaces below. Review any misspelt words 3 times.

LOOK.   SAY.   COVER.   WRITE.   CHECK.

Practise

Practise 1

Practise 2

Practise 3

(TIP) Remember, look up each word in your dictionary to learn its meaning!

Need extra practise?
Printable blank practise sheet available from: www.lifelongeducation.com.au/spelling_practise_sheet
(also available on page 167)

SET 156

Word List

wool	zebra	ate	aloud	got
spent	squirt	stray	sought	thrown
throne	taught	thirst	alert	avenue

INSTRUCTIONS: Review the word list above and then cover. Have someone read out each word while you write them in the spaces below. Review any misspelt words 3 times.

LOOK.   SAY.   COVER.   WRITE.   CHECK.

Practise

Practise 1

Practise 2

Practise 3

TIP Remember, look up each word in your dictionary to learn its meaning!

Need extra practise?
Printable blank practise sheet available from: www.lifelongeducation.com.au/spelling_practise_sheet
(also available on page 167)

Date: ....

Word List

badge	**chose**	**circus**	**cough**	**crane**
cried	**deaf**	**dollar**	**drank**	**feast**
flute	**fried**	**froze**	**grill**	**hatch**

INSTRUCTIONS: Review the word list above and then cover. Have someone read out each word while you write them in the spaces below. Review any misspelt words 3 times.

LOOK.   SAY.   COVER.   WRITE.   CHECK.

Practise

Practise 1

Practise 2

Practise 3

(TIP) Remember, look up each word in your dictionary to learn its meaning!

Need extra practise?
Printable blank practise sheet available from: www.lifelongeducation.com.au/spelling_practise_sheet
(also available on page 167)

SET 158

Word List

hollow	juggle	kept	laid	pebble
poison	riddle	voyage	width	baker
decay	galley	lamb	linen	propel

INSTRUCTIONS: Review the word list above and then cover. Have someone read out each word while you write them in the spaces below. Review any misspelt words 3 times.

LOOK.   SAY.   COVER.   WRITE.   CHECK.

Practise

Practise 1

Practise 2

Practise 3

TIP Remember, look up each word in your dictionary to learn its meaning!

Need extra practise?
Printable blank practise sheet available from: www.lifelongeducation.com.au/spelling_practise_sheet
(also available on page 167)

SET 159

Word List

recess	reign	socket	vacant	vain
veil	vein	ascend	autumn	Monday
bonnet	cement	detach	duet	fasten

INSTRUCTIONS: Review the word list above and then cover. Have someone read out each word while you write them in the spaces below. Review any misspelt words 3 times.

LOOK. SAY. COVER. WRITE. CHECK.

Practise

Practise 1

Practise 2

Practise 3

⬡ TIP Remember, look up each word in your dictionary to learn its meaning!

Need extra practise?
Printable blank practise sheet available from: www.lifelongeducation.com.au/spelling_practise_sheet
(also available on page 167)

SET 160

Date: ....

Word List

collar	abrupt	cuddle	Tuesday	gauge
niece	ninety	obey	puddle	siege
sticky	syrup	waiver	yacht	easier

INSTRUCTIONS: Review the word list above and then cover. Have someone read out each word while you write them in the spaces below. Review any misspelt words 3 times.

LOOK.   SAY.   COVER.   WRITE.   CHECK.

Practise

Practise 1

Practise 2

Practise 3

TIP Remember, look up each word in your dictionary to learn its meaning!

Need extra practise?
Printable blank practise sheet available from: www.lifelongeducation.com.au/spelling_practise_sheet
(also available on page 167)

APPENDIX

PRACTISE SHEET

Lifelong Education
www.lifelongeducation.com.au

Practise 1

Practise 2

Practise 3

Practise 4

Practise 5

Practise 6
